Let's Talk About

BREAKING PROMISES

Let's Talk About
BREAKING PROMISES

By JOY BERRY

Illustrated by John Costanza
Edited by Orly Kelly
Designed by Jill Losson

GROLIER ENTERPRISES CORP.

Let's talk about BREAKING PROMISES.

Have your friends ever disappointed you by not doing something they had told you they would do?

Have grownups ever disappointed you by not doing something they had told you they would do?

When people do not do what they say they will do, they are BREAKING A PROMISE.

When someone breaks a promise —

- how do you feel?
- what do you think?
- what do you do?

When someone breaks a promise —

- you may feel disappointed, frustrated and angry;
- you may think that the person cannot be trusted;
- you may not believe the person the next time he or she makes a promise.

It is important to treat other people the way that you want to be treated.

If you want other people to keep their promises, you will need to keep your promises.

If you keep your promises, people will be able to trust you.

When people trust you —

- they can depend on you, and
  they know that you will not
  let them down;
- they know that you will be honest
  and will not lie.

It is important to have people trust you.

If people trust you —

- they will believe you;
- they will not question or doubt you;
- they will respect you;
- they will allow you to do more on your own.

If you want people to trust you,
you must show them that you
can be trusted.

To show a person that you can be trusted,
be where you say you will be
<u>when</u> you say you will be there.

To show a person that you can be trusted, *do what you say you will do.*

To show a person that you can be trusted,
give what you say you will give.

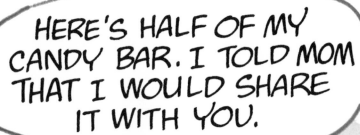

If you want to be trusted, you will need to *keep your promises.*

If you want to be happy, you will treat other people the way you want to be treated.

This means that you will keep your promises because you want other people to keep theirs.